Original title:
Friendship in the Modern World

Copyright © 2024 Swan Charm

Author: Johan Kirsipuu
ISBN HARDBACK: 978-9916-89-037-0
ISBN PAPERBACK: 978-9916-89-038-7
ISBN EBOOK: 978-9916-89-039-4

Multiple Realities, One Heart

In shadows where choices bloom,
Paths intertwine, two souls in gloom.
Echoes of laughter, whispers of fears,
A dance of fate through endless years.

Silent pulses beat in time,
Life's a tapestry, a woven rhyme.
Across the realms, we find our parts,
Multiple stories, but one true heart.

Stars in a Digital Sky

Flickering lights in endless space,
Connections formed, yet lost in place.
Through screens we speak, our voices blend,
Seeking warmth that pixels can't send.

A galaxy spins in coded strokes,
A void of silence 'neath playful jokes.
In this vastness, we seek to fly,
Searching for stars in a digital sky.

Comfort in the Unexpected

A twist of fate, a sudden change,
Life unfolds, both wild and strange.
In chaos found, a gentle peace,
Moments of joy that never cease.

Through open doors we gather round,
Embracing truths in randomness found.
In the unknown, our spirits rise,
Comfort blooms beneath surprise.

Modern Sanctuaries of Connection

In cafés bright, where voices blend,
Strangers meet, and boundaries bend.
With laughter shared and stories told,
Sanctuaries built, both brave and bold.

Online realms where friendships thrive,
A pulse of life, we feel alive.
Connection flows like water's stream,
Modern spaces, a shared dream.

Sketches of Eternity

In whispers drawn upon the night,
Stars weave stories in gentle light.
Time stretches, a canvas unfurled,
Ink of dreams paints the world.

Waves of memory crash on shore,
Echoes linger, forevermore.
Hearts entwined in twilight's glow,
Sketches dance in the ebb and flow.

Colors bleed, the moments blend,
Each stroke a tale, a timeless friend.
The artist's hand, a compass true,
Guides us through the vast and blue.

Fleeting, yet forever they stay,
In every breath, in every sway.
Through shadows deep, a light we find,
Sketches etched in the heart and mind.

As dawn unfolds, the art remains,
In quiet sighs and soft refrains.
Eternity whispers, oh so clear,
In the sketches we hold dear.

Webbed Hearts

Threads of fate, intricately spun,
In the silence, two become one.
Patterns woven, strong and sweet,
Webbed hearts dance in rhythmic beat.

Time stands still, a pause, a breath,
In the tapestry, love finds depth.
Gentle whispers, soft and true,
Every thread leads back to you.

Bound by dreams, we weave our fate,
In every moment, we create.
Through storms and suns, we hold tight,
Webbed hearts shine in the night.

Laughter echoes, threads entwined,
In the fabric of space and time.
Together we soar, never apart,
In the webbed tapestry of the heart.

As shadows shift, our journey flows,
In every heartbeat, love only grows.
With gentle hands, we mend and start,
Forever bound—our webbed hearts.

Soliloquies in Shadows

In corners dim where secrets hide,
The shadows dance, the silence bides.
Whispers echo in the night,
Soliloquies of heart take flight.

A flicker here, a sighing breath,
Each shadow tells of love and death.
In solitude, we find our place,
Where light and dark embrace with grace.

The moon hangs low, a watchful eye,
As dreams of yesterday drift by.
In every crease of twilight's shroud,
Lies the story we've vowed.

Fading moments, bright and dark,
Each soliloquy leaves a mark.
The echoes linger, softly call,
In shadows, we find our all.

As dawn approaches, the quiet stirs,
Whispers of light, the silence blurs.
Still, within, our stories stay,
In soliloquies, night turns to day.

Unseen Handshakes

In the crowd, we pass each other,
A fleeting glance, a silent tether.
Connection blooms without a sound,
Unseen handshakes all around.

Words unsaid in crowded halls,
Echo softly in silent calls.
Hearts aligned in secret trust,
In this moment, we are just.

The air is thick with stories shared,
In every look, a touch declared.
A knot of souls, entwined and free,
In hidden realms, we come to be.

We wander paths of chance and fate,
Each footprint large, though small the gait.
Through the maze of life's demands,
Together still, unseen handshakes stand.

With every step, we learn to see,
The threads of life, connectively.
In whispered dreams, our hopes expand,
In every heart, unseen handshakes planned.

Serendipity in DMs

A message sent, a spark ignites,
In quiet hours, beneath the lights.
Screens reflect a hidden grace,
Serendipity finds its place.

Words flow easy, laughter shared,
In the digital, none compared.
A story lived across the miles,
In silent moments, we share smiles.

Unexpected joys in every text,
In this space, no need to vex.
Connections form with each reply,
In this realm, souls freely fly.

Time dissolves as we connect,
In the quiet, we find respect.
Serendipity in DMs flows,
In every line, our friendship grows.

So here we are, with hearts aligned,
In the realm of thoughts entwined.
Each click, each type, a lucky chance,
Through digital dances, we advance.

Navigating New Currents

The river bends, the water sways,
New currents guide us through the days.
With open hearts, we find our way,
Navigating hope in sweet array.

Each turn brings whispers of the past,
Moments fleeting, yet meant to last.
With every wave, we learn to trust,
In these waters, we adjust.

The sun will set, the stars will gleam,
In this journey, we chase a dream.
With every splash, a story told,
Navigating, brave and bold.

Together, we'll embrace the tide,
With faith that flows, we turn with pride.
Through shifting sands and restless sea,
New currents dance, just you and me.

So let us sail through every storm,
In shared adventure, hearts grow warm.
For every route, the journey's worth,
Navigating life, discovering birth.

Solar Systems of Kindred Spirits

In the cosmos, we align in grace,
Each star reflects a familiar face.
Solar systems swirl, vibrant and bright,
Kindred spirits in the night.

Planets orbit, each path is true,
In shared orbits, I find you.
Galaxies whisper a tale so grand,
In this vastness, together we stand.

Celestial dance, in harmony we flow,
With every heartbeat, our connections grow.
Through nebulae of dreams unfurled,
We find each other in this world.

Eclipses mark the moments we cherish,
In fleeting shadows, friendships nourish.
Solar systems with tales to weave,
Kindred spirits, we believe.

So let us chart our fated skies,
With every twinkle, our love will rise.
In this universe, forever we roam,
Solar systems, our boundless home.

Whispered Secrets in the Cloud

In silence, shadows slide,
Beneath the turquoise sky.
Whispers dance on gentle winds,
Where secrets softly lie.

Among the silver linings,
Dreamers weave their thoughts so light.
Clouds become their canvas,
Painting stories out of sight.

Every drop, a memory,
Each breeze, a soothing balm.
In twilight's shimmering glow,
Hearts find their quiet calm.

With every gust, they gather,
Sharing tales of distant lands.
In the mist, all is possible,
Connected, hand in hand.

So let the whispers linger,
As constellations play.
In the cloud where love resides,
Forever we shall stay.

Ties that Transcend Timezones

With every sunrise dawning,
A bond grows strong and true.
Miles apart, yet beating hearts,
Feel the love that's due.

Through the hours shifting slowly,
We write our letters bold.
Each word a bridge connecting,
More precious than fine gold.

The clock may tick and shimmer,
But time cannot confine.
For every laugh we share,
Creates a line divine.

So when the night enfolds us,
And distance seems so far,
Just look into the starlight,
And know where you are.

In dreams, we meet together,
Through each sweet, silent hour.
Our ties, they stretch like rivers,
A testament of power.

The Art of Staying Close

In moments small and fleeting,
We make our hearts align.
A smile, a text, a gesture,
Transforming space and time.

The world can pull us further,
Yet love knows not a chain.
With every thought and heartbeat,
Together, we remain.

In laughter and in silence,
We find our sacred space.
Distance fades with every glance,
In memory's warm embrace.

We cherish each connection,
A thread that will not sever.
In the art of staying close,
We craft our bonds forever.

So when the shadows lengthen,
And paths seem far apart,
Know I'll be there beside you,
In the corners of your heart.

Navigating the Cyber Sea

In networks wide and wondrous,
We sail through waves of light.
With pixels as our vessels,
We chart a course so bright.

Connected by the currents,
We ride the tides of thought.
Each click, a whispered message,
In every link, we're caught.

We traverse quiet harbors,
And plunge in stormy skies.
Yet hand in digital hand,
We rise as daylight cries.

With every post and story,
Our hearts begin to blend.
In this vast, virtual ocean,
You'll always be my friend.

So let the screens surround us,
Their glow, our guiding star.
Together through this cyber sea,
No distance feels too far.

Bonds Beyond Borders

Across wide seas, we share a dream,
With whispered hopes that softly gleam.
Though miles apart, our hearts entwined,
In every beat, connection aligned.

In letters penned, emotions flow,
A bridge of words in the moon's glow.
Cultures blend in laughter's song,
In the tapestry of life, we belong.

Through storms we brave, the distance grows,
Yet in our hearts, the warmth still glows.
With every message, a thread so fine,
Binding souls as if divine.

We dance with shadows in the night,
Awakening love in shared twilight.
No borders can confine our ties,
For love transcends, and never dies.

Together we rise, hand in hand,
No matter where we make our stand.
Time may part, but love stays true,
In every heart, I find you too.

Conversations at Midnight

In the stillness, our voices meet,
With whispered dreams, soft and sweet.
The clock ticks slow, the stars align,
In shadows deep, our thoughts combine.

Every secret finds its way,
As twilight fades into the gray.
The world outside fades to the past,
In midnight chats, our souls are cast.

With laughter shared, fears take flight,
In gentle tones, we find our light.
Each word a spark, igniting the night,
In this cocoon, everything feels right.

Moments linger, wrapped in time,
As hearts converse in rhythm and rhyme.
The dawn may come, but we hold fast,
In every silence, our bond amassed.

So let the hours softly wane,
In each exchange, we'll never feign.
For in this space, forever true,
The world is ours, just me and you.

Heartbeats in the Cloud

Floating high, where dreams reside,
In silver lines, our hopes abide.
With every pulse, we intertwine,
In digital realms, our souls align.

Lost in time, yet never far,
Our laughter echoes like a star.
In every heartbeat, presence feels,
As love transcends what life reveals.

Clouds may part and shadows fall,
But in our hearts, we conquer all.
With every message sent anew,
A spark ignites, forever true.

In dreams we chase, the skies extend,
Where distant souls can still transcend.
Together we soar, through every doubt,
In every heartbeat, love's about.

So take my hand in this soft haze,
We'll dance amidst these gentle waves.
For in this space, our hearts reside,
In beats and rhythms, side by side.

Virtual Embraces

In pixels bright, your smile beams,
Through glass, we share our wildest dreams.
In every chat, a warmth we find,
An embrace that knows no bind.

With words exchanged, our souls connect,
In this vast world, what we expect.
Through screens we reach, and hearts take flight,
In every moment, love feels right.

The distance fades, as time holds still,
In every laugh, a sweet thrill.
With virtual hugs that warmly flow,
In silent spaces, feelings grow.

Though physical touch may not be near,
In every glance, our hearts draw near.
Together we'll craft this dream we chase,
In every click, I find your grace.

So let the miles stretch out wide,
In this virtual realm, I'll be your guide.
For in this space, love finds its place,
In every heartbeat, a warm embrace.

Trust in Taps

Fingers dance on glowing glass,
Whispers shared, moments pass.
With each tap, a bond we weave,
Silent truths, we dare believe.

Through the screen, we find our way,
Guided by the words we say.
Trust is born with every click,
Paths converge, connections thick.

In the chaos, calm we seek,
Every message, strong yet meek.
Hopes entwined in pixel light,
Hearts in sync, we hold on tight.

Yet in shadows, doubt can creep,
Vulnerable, our secrets keep.
But faith ignites with every share,
Building bridges in the air.

So let us tap, let us share,
In this dance, we lay us bare.
For every trust can find its way,
In the rhythm of the day.

Unforgettable Uploads

Images splash across the screen,
Moments captured, pure and keen.
Each upload tells a tale so bright,
Memories crafted, hearts take flight.

In the pixels, laughter dwells,
Stories woven, magic spells.
With every post, we come alive,
In this space, our dreams derive.

Scrolling back, we find our past,
Each snapshot, a moment cast.
Fragile joys, our hearts embrace,
In this digital, sacred space.

Echoes linger, whispers heard,
In the noise, a soft word.
Unforgettable, they fill our days,
Guiding us through myriad ways.

So upload, share, let love unfold,
In every story, be bold.
For in the web we frame our lives,
Unforgettable, how it thrives.

The Warmth of Glowing Screens

At dusk, they glow with gentle light,
Comfort found in the silent night.
In every pixel, warmth remains,
A soft embrace that breaks the chains.

Fingers glide, connections spark,
We share our dreams, ignite the dark.
Through the glow, we find our peace,
Moments captured never cease.

While worlds apart, we feel so near,
In laughter shared, in every tear.
Here we build our sacred space,
A tapestry of love and grace.

Yet, in shadows, caution lingers,
Navigating with tender fingers.
For in this warmth, we seek the true,
Heartfelt gestures, just me and you.

So let the screens illuminate,
The love we share, our destined fate.
For in this light, we find our way,
The warmth grows stronger every day.

Connection Without Conditions

In a world of endless scroll,
We seek to find a common goal.
Connection blooms, roots intertwine,
In every heartbeat, love aligns.

No strings attached, no need to impress,
Every soul, we learn to bless.
In shared thoughts, we find our grace,
Embracing all, in this vast space.

With open hearts, we journey far,
Guided by each shining star.
In laughter's echo, we come alive,
Together, through all we strive.

Trust unspoken, a bond so deep,
In every moment, love we keep.
No conditions, just genuine care,
In this realm, our souls laid bare.

So join me in this timeless dance,
In the freedom of our chance.
For connections grow with each embrace,
Without conditions, we find our place.

Heartfelt Bytes

In the quiet hum of night,
Whispers weave through pixel light.
Each message holds a spark of grace,
Threads of love we softly trace.

Moments shared in silent text,
A bond that time cannot perplex.
Emojis dance like stars above,
Pixelated proof of love.

Fingers tap, hearts open wide,
In this world, there's none to hide.
Through screens, we send our dreams so true,
Every byte speaks just of you.

Listening close to every sound,
In every byte, our hearts are bound.
A simple link, yet so profound,
In digital, our love is found.

Together in this space we share,
Digital threads, a lovely snare.
In the vastness, we collide,
Heartfelt bytes will be our guide.

Constellations of Companionship

Underneath the velvet sky,
Stars align and spirits fly.
Each twinkle tells a tale of old,
A friendship forged in warmth, not cold.

Like constellations shining bright,
We find our way through darkest night.
Guiding lights that never fade,
In every heart, foundations laid.

Bonded in this cosmic dance,
Every glance holds a chance.
Through time and space, we intertwine,
Together, our stars brightly shine.

From whispered dreams to laughter shared,
Each moment lived, with love declared.
In this vastness, souls ignite,
Constellations glow, hearts take flight.

In the tapestry of night,
We find each other, hold on tight.
Celebrating every spark's embrace,
In companionship, we find our place.

Resiliency in the Feed

Amidst the storms of highs and lows,
The feed flows on, resilience grows.
With every scroll, we find the fight,
Voices rise, igniting light.

Stories shared, and hearts laid bare,
In unity, we find repair.
With laughter, tears, and hope in sight,
Together, we stand firm and bright.

Through trials faced and battles won,
Each post a thread, we weave as one.
In digital realms, our dreams take flight,
Resiliency shines, a beacon of light.

For every struggle shared, a hand,
In a world so vast, we understand.
Our spirits soar as we exceed,
In every share, there's strength to lead.

So let the feed roll on and on,
In every echo, we are drawn.
Through every challenge, we will meet,
Together, we rise, and none retreat.

Cryptic Messages of Care

In the silence, whispers flow,
Hidden truths in shadows grow.
Messages wrapped in gentle grace,
Cryptic signs of love's embrace.

A glance exchanged, a fleeting smile,
Moments paused, a loving while.
In every look, a story shared,
Each tiny act, a heart laid bare.

In coded words, we subtly speak,
Deepened bonds, no need for seek.
Every gesture, soft and rare,
Unveiling secrets we both share.

Though unspoken, feelings roam,
In the quiet, you feel like home.
In every silence, love declares,
These cryptic messages of care.

With every heartbeat, we discern,
In each mystery, love will burn.
A language spoken, pure and fair,
In the stillness, tender care.

Kindness in the Scroll

In the quiet of the night,
Words can heal or ignite.
A gentle touch on the screen,
Kindness flows, soft and keen.

Echoes travel far and wide,
Bridging hearts, side by side.
In the labyrinth of the mind,
Hope and love are intertwined.

Each message like a seed,
Sown with care, planted with heed.
A simple phrase can uplift,
Transforming shadows into gift.

Through the shadows, light can pour,
With every heart that we restore.
Kindness in the scroll we write,
Guides us through the darkest night.

So let's nurture every word,
Let compassion be our sword.
In this world of click and scroll,
We can make a kinder whole.

Umbrellas of Understanding

Under storms that rage and sway,
We seek shelter in the fray.
Umbrellas raised, we stand as one,
In the chaos, hope's begun.

Each canopy holds a tale,
Sharing voices, someone's mail.
Together we can face the rain,
United, we shall bear the strain.

With colors bright against the gray,
Bearing love in soft array.
Individual yet combined,
A tapestry of hearts aligned.

In the downpour, we will learn,
How to heal and how to yearn.
With every drop that falls in time,
We'll make trust our paradigm.

As the clouds begin to part,
We find solace in each heart.
Umbrellas of understanding wide,
Sheltering hope, side by side.

Gathering the Digital Harvest

In fields of virtual light,
We sow dreams both day and night.
Gathering crops that wisdom sows,
In the harvest, kindness grows.

Each click a seed of thought,
Nurtured by the love we've sought.
Connected minds, a thriving share,
Bringing forth the fruits of care.

In the click and scroll we find,
A wealth of hearts and open minds.
From every corner, every land,
We cultivate what is truly grand.

Let us reap what we have sown,
In this garden we have grown.
A tapestry of varied hues,
Gathered with the bonds we choose.

Sharing knowledge, sharing fate,
In unity we celebrate.
Harvest moments intertwined,
Digital love, a true gold mine.

Cherished Clicks

In the rhythm of our days,
Through the web's unfocused maze.
Cherished clicks and gentle swipes,
Capture laughter, capture gripes.

Every like a fleeting trace,
Ties us all in this shared space.
With each touch, a bond is formed,
In this realm, we're all transformed.

Moments shared from far and near,
Whispers soft, yet crystal clear.
Each click a portal, love confined,
In memories that still unwind.

Through the pixels, tales unfold,
Stories waiting to be told.
Cherished moments, never lost,
Connections made at any cost.

So here's to every gentle press,
In this space we find our stress.
Cherished clicks that weave our fate,
In this bond, we celebrate.

Handwritten Notes in Texts

Pen strokes dance on a page,
Whispers caught in fleeting words.
Ink spills tales of yesterday,
Heartfelt feelings, softly stirred.

Fingers glide on glassy screens,
Messages, a balm for souls.
Lost in thoughts and quiet dreams,
Connection finds its subtle roles.

Notes tucked safe within our minds,
Each syllable a cherished sound.
Silent moments, laughter binds,
In the chaos, peace is found.

Shadows linger in the air,
Each emoji, a smile shared.
Despite the distance, we both care,
Through these lines, our hearts are bared.

Tender echoes fill the night,
Every text a warm embrace.
In this world of black and white,
Love still leaves a handwritten trace.

In Each Other's Orbit

Two souls drift through starry skies,
Gravitational pull at play.
In your light, my spirit flies,
Every glance, a warm ballet.

Thoughts collide like meteors bright,
In our dance, we find our way.
Across the cosmos, pure delight,
In this rhythm, we both sway.

Every heartbeat draws us near,
Waves of warmth, a soft embrace.
Whispers echo, crystal clear,
Together in our sacred space.

Celestial paths intertwine,
Through the void, our love will soar.
In your arms, I feel divine,
Endless dreams, forevermore.

Orbits join as time goes by,
Like stars that twinkle in the night.
Hand in hand, we mesmerize,
Bound in love, a cosmic flight.

Moments Between Notifications

Silence hums between each ping,
Breath held tight, anticipation.
In stillness, hearts begin to sing,
Life's simple, pure sensation.

A glance exchanged, a knowing smile,
Between the buzz, a sacred pause.
In these moments, we reconcile,
Finding peace within the noise.

Time stretches thin, then breaks apart,
Every laugh, a fleeting spark.
In this world, we play our part,
Holding joy within the dark.

Notifications come and go,
But these minutes hold a glow.
In the quiet, love will grow,
In between, our hearts will flow.

Cherished seconds, soft and sweet,
A treasure found in each delay.
In your eyes, my heart's retreat,
Moments live where words decay.

Unseen Threads

Woven strands connect our hearts,
Invisible but oh so strong.
In the quiet, love imparts,
A melody, our whispered song.

Flickering lights from dawn till dusk,
In the shadows, secrets hide.
Through every trial, every trust,
These threads bind us, side by side.

Gentle tugs pull at our fate,
In the chaos, we align.
Unraveling, we ponder wait,
For in patience, love will shine.

Every choice, a line we weave,
Intricate paths, forever near.
In each sigh, we dare believe,
Unseen threads whisper, "I'm here."

Though unseen, our hearts are known,
Through the distance, love will thread.
In every glance, seeds are sown,
A tapestry in which we tread.

Virtual Embraces

In a world of screens, we connect,
With every message, we reflect.
Hearts are shared through pixels bright,
A warm embrace in digital light.

Through wired words, our dreams unfold,
In softest whispers, secrets told.
Though miles apart, we hold so near,
Our laughter echoes, crystal clear.

Each click and tap, a bond we weave,
In this vast space, we do believe.
Together alone, we find our way,
In virtual halls where we choose to stay.

A glowing screen holds you so tight,
As we dance together in the night.
In every smile, we bridge the gap,
In this embrace of love's sweet map.

So here we stand, two souls online,
In every heartbeat, we intertwine.
With every chat, we softly grace,
The beauty found in virtual embrace.

Kindred Spirits Online

A click of keys, a world unfolds,
In forums bright, our stories told.
Kindred spirits, though far apart,
In every post, we feel the heart.

Thread by thread, we weave our tales,
In laughter shared, where joy prevails.
Across the globe, our voices blend,
In unity, our souls ascend.

Through midnight chats and morning light,
We hold each other, spirits bright.
In shared adventures, dreams take flight,
In this vast web, we find our light.

Every emoji, a smile sent,
In every moment, time is spent.
Though screens divide, we come alive,
In this connection, we truly thrive.

Together, we unlock the door,
To every heart, we will explore.
Kindred spirits, forever aligned,
In this digital world, our hearts combined.

Joy in the Byte

In every byte, a spark ignites,
With laughter shared on starry nights.
Through screens we glimpse a world anew,
In every word, we find what's true.

Joy flows freely in online streams,
In endless chats, we chase our dreams.
Amidst the noise, a chorus sings,
In rhythmic pulses, love takes wings.

With every post, a little light,
In threads of hope, we find our sight.
A pixel here, a moment there,
Together, we breathe this virtual air.

Friendship blooms within the code,
In every link, a shared abode.
Across the vast and endless space,
In joy we meet, in love's embrace.

So let us dance in this delight,
In every laugh, in every byte.
Together we paint this vibrant scene,
With joy à la mode, forever keen.

A Network of Souls

A web of hearts, a network spun,
Across the world, we have begun.
In every chat, a spark ignites,
A tapestry of pure delights.

We share our hopes, our dreams align,
Through every message, hearts entwine.
In this connection, deep and real,
A bond of souls, a shared appeal.

Through all the highs and every low,
In silent hugs, we let love flow.
With every pixel, our spirits soar,
In this vast realm, we crave for more.

With laughter bright and kindness shared,
In every moment, we have dared.
To bridge the gaps that life bestows,
In this network, every heart knows.

So here's to us, to all we've found,
In every word, love's echo sound.
A network strong, forever whole,
In unity, we find our soul.

Navigating New Horizons

With every dawn, a chance to rise,
New paths to walk beneath the skies.
The map is drawn, but wide the space,
Adventure calls in every place.

Into the wild, our spirits leap,
Through fields of gold and mountains steep.
With hearts aflame, we chase the sun,
Together here, we journey on.

The winds of change will guide our way,
Through storms and calm, come what may.
With open minds, we'll learn and grow,
In every step, our spirit flows.

The stars align, we dare to dream,
With every whisper from the stream.
Each moment shines, a gem so bright,
We'll find our paths, embrace the light.

So here we stand on this new shore,
With courage, love, we seek for more.
In every heartbeat, worlds will blend,
New horizons, with each friend.

The Language of Our Times

In words we weave, a tale so bold,
A symphony of stories told.
With every laugh and sorrow shared,
A bond is forged, a dream declared.

We speak in memes, in texts we find,
Expressions shift, yet hearts align.
A growing lexicon for all,
In every tweet, we rise and fall.

The rhythm beats in pulsing tones,
Our hearts converse through digital phones.
In every voice, a tale is spun,
A language forged, we all are one.

Through screens we reach, across the miles,
Connecting souls with shared smiles.
In hashtags bright, our hopes unite,
Together strong, igniting light.

So let us speak without retreat,
In every word, our lives complete.
The language blooms, a bond so strong,
In every voice, we all belong.

Shared Dreams in a Click

In an instant, dreams take flight,
A world transformed by shared delight.
With every click, a vision glows,
Connected hearts where magic flows.

Ideas spark in vibrant streams,
Collaboration births our dreams.
With every post, we build a fate,
Unified, we elevate.

The canvas wide, our brush in hand,
Together painting futures grand.
In forums loud, our voices rise,
New hopes ignite beneath the skies.

From distant shores, we echo loud,
In unity, we stand proud.
With laughter shared and tears we mend,
Our dreams extend, as realms blend.

Each moment counts, each click a chance,
To weave together this great dance.
In every heart, a dream so bold,
In clicks, our stories will unfold.

Jokes in the Ether

In silent whispers, laughter grows,
A playful spark in soft repose.
With every poke, the humor flows,
In jests and puns, the joy bestows.

From chat rooms bright to memes divine,
In pixels glint, we draw the line.
A joke in ether, light as air,
It travels far, beyond compare.

In every chuckle, bonds are made,
With silly tales that never fade.
Together we laugh, a shared delight,
In gleeful moments, hearts take flight.

So let us share a smile today,
In every jest, we find our way.
For laughter heals, unites us all,
With jokes aloft, like leaves that fall.

In the ether's dance, we're never alone,
For every laugh, a seed is sown.
In punchlines bright, our spirits soar,
A lightness found, forevermore.

The Bond Beyond Borders

Across the ocean wide and deep,
Friendship blooms, its roots run steep.
Miles may part, but hearts unite,
In whispers soft, through day and night.

Language may differ, cultures sway,
Yet love transcends in its own way.
Hand in hand, though far apart,
We share our dreams, we share our heart.

Through every storm, we stand as one,
Under the same moon, same sun.
Distance shrinks when spirits soar,
In every laugh, we find much more.

In darkest hours, in brightest days,
The bond we share, it never sways.
Though borders may bind, our souls are free,
Together forever, just you and me.

So here's to us, to paths we weave,
In every moment, we believe.
A tapestry made of love so true,
The bond beyond borders, me and you.

Hearts Unplugged

In a world of noise, we seek the calm,
With simple joys, and nature's balm.
Two souls connect without the screen,
In moments shared, where love is keen.

A soft breeze whispers through the trees,
Hand in hand, we find our ease.
Conversations flow, no rush, no time,
In every laugh, our hearts must chime.

Forget the buzz, forget the likes,
In shared silence, our spirit strikes.
Eyes that sparkle, smiles that gleam,
Unplugged, we dance within a dream.

Under the stars, our worries fade,
In the glow of night, we've gently played.
The world awaits, yet here we stay,
In our haven, we find our way.

Tomorrow comes, and life moves fast,
But this moment, we'll make it last.
With hearts in sync, like a rhythmic song,
Together, forever, where we belong.

When Screens Fade Away

As twilight falls and light grows dim,
We turn the page, let memories swim.
In the quiet space where silence dwells,
We breathe in life, no need for bells.

The world outside can wait a while,
In your presence, I find my smile.
No vibrant screens to steal the view,
Just me and you, in shades of blue.

Each tick of time, a treasure known,
In whispered truths, our love has grown.
When screens fade away, hearts take flight,
In the dark, we find our light.

The laughter shared, the stories spun,
Reminds us both of where we're from.
With each heartbeat, we paint the sky,
When screens fade away, we learn to fly.

So let us cherish this sacred space,
With every glance, we feel the grace.
For in our dreams, we'll always stay,
When screens fade away, our love will play.

Shared Solitude

In quiet corners, where shadows blend,
We find a solace, an unspoken friend.
Two hearts that beat in tranquil tune,
Under the watch of the silver moon.

In moments still, when time stands bare,
We weave our thoughts in the evening air.
Solitude shared, in whispers low,
A gentle bond, it starts to grow.

No need for words, no grand display,
In silent company, we find our way.
The world outside can ebb and flow,
In shared solitude, love will glow.

A sip of tea, a book in hand,
In simple pleasures, we understand.
Together alone, in this lovely space,
Where calm embraces, we find our place.

So here we sit, two souls entwined,
In the depth of peace, our hearts aligned.
For solitude shared is never bleak,
In the calm embrace, our spirits speak.

Bonds Beyond the Blue Light

In the glow of the screen, we connect,
Words shared and dreams intersect.
Though miles apart, we're never alone,
In digital realms, our spirits have grown.

Whispers of laughter dance in the air,
Echoes of friendship, a bond we share.
Moments captured in pixels and sound,
In this vast web, our hearts are unbound.

Through trials and joys, we stand side by side,
A network of trust where love can't hide.
Beyond the distance, through every fight,
We forge our paths in the soft blue light.

Each message a thread, weaving us tight,
Tales of our journeys, our shared delight.
In bytes and bits, our stories unfold,
A tapestry rich, with colors bold.

So here's to the bonds that distance can't sever,
Connections like stars, shining forever.
In the heart of the world, our voices unite,
Together we thrive, beyond the blue light.

More Than a Click

A single click awakens the space,
Bridging the gaps, a virtual trace.
Fingers dance lightly across the keys,
With every message, we share the breeze.

From distant lands, we hear the call,
A community built, the rise and fall.
With every post, our lives intertwine,
Stories shared, like aged, fine wine.

In hashtags and threads, we find our way,
Morning sun or evening gray.
For deeper than clicks, our hearts align,
In a world where distance feels less confined.

Communities form in the strangest of ways,
In digital fields, we spend our days.
Through laughter and tears, together we stand,
In pixels and dreams, we make our own land.

So let us embrace this realm we create,
Each click and each tap, a bond so innate.
In this vast network, we're never alone,
More than a click, we've built our home.

Kinship in the Feed

Scroll through the feed, what stories we find,
Echoes of laughter, hearts intertwined.
In snapshots of life, our journeys unfold,
Each moment a treasure, a memory to hold.

Through trials and triumphs, we share our truth,
Wisdom in words, the spark of our youth.
In comments and likes, we build our refrain,
A kinship robust, through joy and through pain.

From memes that inspire to tears that we shed,
In this virtual space, we're brightly led.
Through struggles and victories, we stand as one,
In the vibrant mesh, our souls have begun.

Each post a reminder of humanity's grace,
In this fast-paced world, we find our place.
A tapestry woven through laughter and tears,
In digital kinship, we quell all our fears.

So scroll on with purpose, connect and engage,
In this boundless space, together we wage.
For every like shared, a bond stronger brewed,
In the feed of our lives, we're forever imbued.

Navigation through Noise

In the chaos of voices, we find our own,
Amidst the clamor, new seeds are sown.
With whispers of wisdom guiding our way,
We navigate through the murmur each day.

Tides of information wash over our shore,
Yet through the noise, we search for more.
For clarity blooms in the heart's quiet space,
When we pause and reflect, we find our place.

Links and likes may drown out the real,
But in the stillness, our truths we reveal.
In moments of doubt, we stand tall and bold,
Navigating through what the world has told.

So listen intently, let silence speak,
Amongst the distractions, find what you seek.
For connection thrives when we trust our own voice,
Amidst all the noise, let's make the choice.

Together we journey, hand in hand,
Through the labyrinth of stories, we understand.
In the delicate silence, our paths align true,
In navigation through noise, I walk with you.

Diaries of the Distant

In quiet corners, thoughts reside,
Old whispers echo, dreams collide.
Pages turn, a silent grace,
Time unfolds a distant place.

Faded ink on weathered leaves,
Stories linger where heart believes.
Moments trapped within the text,
Memories dwindle, dreams perplexed.

Letters stained with longing's hue,
A bond woven with thoughts anew.
Beneath the stars, we write and share,
In every dark, we find a prayer.

Each diary page, a fragile thread,
Connecting hearts long left unsaid.
With every line, space disappears,
Together still, despite the years.

Distant dreams, yet close we stand,
In written words, we hold a hand.
Through shadows cast by fleeting times,
We find our truth in silent rhymes.

Colorful Solitudes

In gardens filled with hues so bright,
A tapestry of day and night.
Petals whisper, soft and low,
Alone they dance, yet steal the show.

Colors swirl in gentle breeze,
Each a note that aims to please.
Solitudes in vibrant play,
Finding peace in shades of gray.

A canvas wide, each stroke distinct,
Lives apart, yet hearts are linked.
Moments pause to watch and stare,
In every hue, a love we share.

Reflection pools in quiet streams,
Where solitude blooms and gleams.
Amidst the space, we quietly grow,
In colorful dreams, we come to know.

With every shade, our spirits rise,
In solitude, we find surprise.
From lonely tones, a symphony,
In vivid hearts, we're truly free.

Together in Separation

Two souls dance on a thread so fine,
Carved from the air, a love divine.
Each heartbeat carries distant songs,
In silent spaces, where love belongs.

Miles apart, yet close we hold,
Stories shared, often told.
In shadows cast by longing light,
Together in dreams, we take flight.

A whisper shared across the void,
Echoes of joy that can't be destroyed.
In every sunset, we feel the tie,
Together we rise, together we sigh.

In pages turned, our paths align,
Drawing hope from the subtle sign.
Though often worlds divide our ways,
In separation, love always stays.

With threads unseen, our lives entwine,
A bond so strong, it won't decline.
In every moment that time won't sever,
We are together, now and forever.

Navigating New Friendships

In laughter shared, connections bloom,
New bonds form, dispelling gloom.
Paths entwine in joy's embrace,
Each story shared, a sacred space.

With open hearts, we take the dive,
In every moment, we feel alive.
Together we stumble, together we rise,
In laughter and tears, we find our ties.

In shared adventures, trust begins,
As light breaks through, the darkness thins.
Navigating roads less well known,
In friendship's light, we find our home.

Through quiet chats and starry nights,
We weave our dreams, we share our sights.
In every heartbeat, values blend,
Together we grow, together we mend.

With every step, new paths we trace,
In the tapestry of time and space.
In the journey of souls, hand in hand,
Navigating new friendships, where we stand.

Map of Untold Stories

A map of whispers, secrets bare,
In every fold, a tale to share.
Lines that dance, lost and found,
In shadows deep, where dreams surround.

Each mark a heart, a moment's grace,
Tracing paths through time and space.
Winding roads, a journey sought,
In ink of courage, battles fought.

Beneath the stars, a guiding light,
Illuminating the dark of night.
With every step, the stories blend,
A tapestry that knows no end.

A silent voice in winds that blow,
Whispers of places we long to go.
In every crease, a life's refrain,
Map of stories, joy, and pain.

So take this map, embrace the call,
In every journey, we rise, we fall.
Through unknown lands, we pave the way,
A map of hearts, forever stay.

Safe Havens in Transmission

In quiet rooms where hearts collide,
Whispers echo, love is our guide.
Safe havens in the storm's embrace,
Two souls find shelter, a sacred space.

Messages travel on waves of trust,
In shared silence, we learn, we must.
Found in laughter, tears that flow,
Safe havens shine, a tranquil glow.

Between the lines, connection grows,
Understanding blooms like flowers' prose.
Across the distance, we paint our dreams,
In every heartbeat, a love that beams.

Through the static, our voices ring,
A symphony of hope we bring.
In the chaos, we find our song,
Safe havens hold us where we belong.

So hold me close, let the world fade,
In this journey, together we wade.
Safe havens built on love's foundation,
Forever in our hearts, transmission.

Discovering Each Other

In a crowded room, eyes meet shy,
Silent questions spark and fly.
Words unspoken, feelings rise,
Discovering each other, beneath the skies.

With every glance, a story shared,
In simple gestures, love is declared.
From laughter's light to whispered fears,
Discovering each other, through the years.

Paths intertwine like vines that grow,
In hidden corners, hearts will show.
Finding comfort in shared delight,
Discovering each other through the night.

Underneath the stars, we dance so free,
In quiet moments, just you and me.
Every heartbeat brings us closer still,
Discovering each other, a timeless thrill.

As seasons change and time unfolds,
Richer treasures than golds and molds.
In every memory, love's sweet glow,
Discovering each other, we always know.

Beyond the Limiting Frame

Caught in the edges of frames too tight,
We dream in colors that spark the night.
Beyond the limits where shadows dwell,
Lies a horizon in freedom's swell.

Each boundary fades with a brave new thought,
In the light of visions that can't be bought.
Breaking free from society's maze,
Beyond the limiting frame, we blaze.

With every step into the unknown,
We carve our paths, no longer alone.
Unchained from doubt, we soar like the breeze,
Beyond the limiting frame, we find our ease.

In hearts unbound, creativity sings,
A world of wonders and daring things.
With courage deep, in unity's name,
Beyond the limiting frame, we reclaim.

So let us rise, hand in hand,
Exploring places, unplanned, unplanned.
For in our journey, we find the same,
Beyond the limiting frame, we proclaim.

In Between Words

In whispers soft, they dance and sway,
A silence shared, yet here to stay.
Unspoken thoughts that linger near,
The space between, so crystal clear.

Through the cracks, emotions spill,
With every pause, an aching thrill.
The heart conveys what words can't say,
In glances lost, we find our way.

A heavy gaze, a fleeting glance,
In that moment, a fleeting chance.
Connections forged in quiet storms,
In between words, our spirit warms.

With each heartbeat, we draw close,
A language formed, yet never chose.
The stories weave, the feelings blend,
In between words, we make amends.

So let the silence talk anew,
In every pause, love's language grew.
Amidst the noise, we find our tune,
In words unspoken, hearts attune.

Laughter Across Time Zones

Echoes of joy like distant chimes,
Resonate through the seams of time.
From dusk till dawn, we share a laugh,
Uniting souls on a vibrant path.

Across the miles, the smiles stream,
Moments crafted like a dream.
In every giggle, warmth ignites,
A bridge connecting our long nights.

The clocks may clash, yet spirits align,
In each chuckle, a softened line.
We break the distance with our cheer,
Through laughter's echo, hearts draw near.

A world apart, but never alone,
In mirthful tales, our bonds have grown.
With every joke, a thread we weave,
Together still, we dare believe.

So let the laughter cross the skies,
Igniting joy where friendship lies.
In every time zone, love adheres,
Through laughter shared, we conquer fears.

Remnants of Yesterday's Echoes

In corners dim, where shadows fell,
The past resides, a whispered spell.
Memories linger, haunt and play,
In remnants traced, by light of day.

Ghostly laughter drifts on air,
A fleeting touch, a tender care.
In every corner, stories bloom,
Yet linger still in haunted rooms.

Faded photographs tell the tale,
Of joy and sorrow, smiles and frail.
Each silent scream and joyful glance,
In echoes past, we find our dance.

Time slips by, yet shadows cling,
To memories that we still bring.
In echoes soft, we find our way,
To yesterday's light in shades of gray.

So let us listen to the flow,
Of yesterday's whispers, soft and low.
In remnants found, our spirits soar,
In echoes past, we are once more.

Embracing the Invisible

In every breath, a presence felt,
In quiet moments, our senses melt.
The unseen threads that weave us tight,
In shadows cast, we hold the light.

Connections deep, though out of sight,
In hidden realms, we find our might.
With every heartbeat, softly thrum,
Embracing what can't be undone.

The gentle touch of a distant star,
Guides our hearts, no matter how far.
In whispers soft, the truth resides,
In invisible bonds, love abides.

We dance on edges of what we know,
In unseen realms, we bravely grow.
With open hearts, we seek and find,
The beauty found in the unconfined.

So let us cherish the unseen grace,
In every moment, a warm embrace.
In invisible love, we share a dream,
In every heartbeat, a sacred theme.

Threads of Humanity

In every heart, a story waits,
Weave your dreams through open gates.
Together we walk this ancient road,
Hand in hand, sharing each load.

Voices rise in the quiet night,
Echoes of love, a guiding light.
Bound by threads of joy and pain,
In unity, we break each chain.

Through storms and trials, we remain,
Sewn together in joy and strain.
Every fabric tells a tale,
In humanity, we shall prevail.

With every glance, connection grows,
In laughter and tears, our essence flows.
Threads of hope intertwine us all,
Together we rise, together we fall.

In the tapestry of life we dwell,
Woven dreams, we craft and tell.
Though colors fade and time may fray,
Humanity's thread will never stray.

The Pulse of Shared Experience

In every laugh, a spark ignites,
Shared moments soar to dizzy heights.
The pulse beats strong, a rhythm shared,
In every gaze, our souls are bared.

Together we face the rising sun,
Through highs and lows, we have begun.
The pulse of life flows deep and wide,
In every heartbeat, we confide.

As seasons change and time rolls on,
In every dusk, a new dawn.
Connections forged in the fire of life,
Through joy and sorrow, through peace and strife.

Each story told, a thread we spin,
In the tapestry, we all fit in.
A mosaic bright, of hopes and fears,
The pulse of shared experience appears.

So let us dance together free,
In the pulse of life, just you and me.
Shared laughter rings in every place,
Together we find our sacred space.

Brightening Distant Days

In twilight moments, dreams take flight,
Guiding stars shine in the night.
Whispers of hope across the skies,
Bringing light where darkness lies.

As dawn unfolds in golden hue,
Every heart awakens anew.
Brightening distant days ahead,
With every word that's kindly said.

In gentle breezes, love will flow,
Seeds of kindness we will sow.
Each smile shared, a radiant ray,
Illuminating life's vast array.

Through storms we weather, hand in hand,
Together we rise, together we stand.
Brightening paths that once were dim,
In unity, our chances brim.

So hold on tightly, dreamers bold,
For every day, a tale unfolds.
In distant days, our hearts will stay,
Brightening lives in every way.

Unraveled Connections

Threads unspooled, stories once sealed,
In whispers shared, our fates revealed.
Unraveled bonds through time and space,
Finding meaning in every trace.

Every heartbeat, a gentle pull,
Echoes of love, endlessly full.
Connections made in laughter's embrace,
In every meeting, every space.

Through tangled paths, we learn and grow,
In every parting, seeds we sow.
Unraveled connections, woven tight,
A tapestry of shared delight.

As we journey, the threads remain,
Binding us close through joy and pain.
Each story shared, a guiding hand,
Together we rise, together we stand.

Let love lead through the twists and turns,
In every heart, a passion burns.
Unraveled connections, forever strong,
In the chorus of life, we all belong.

Backlit Bonds

In the glow of screens, we find our place,
Soft whispers shared, a warm embrace.
Connections forged in pixel light,
Together we stand, though miles out of sight.

Through streaming songs and laughter loud,
We build our world, a glowing crowd.
Each notification, a sweet delight,
Backlit bonds bloom in the darkest night.

A virtual touch, a heartbeat shared,
Filling the void, showing we cared.
In the realm of bytes, our dreams take flight,
With ever-growing love, our hearts ignite.

Even as shadows may start to creep,
We find our joy in bonds we keep.
In every photo, a story told,
Backlit bonds that never grow old.

So let us cherish this unique dance,
A tapestry woven through chance and glance.
In digital worlds, our spirits soar,
Backlit bonds forevermore.

Tuning Into Togetherness

In harmony, we find our tune,
Voices blend, like stars in June.
Together we laugh, together we sigh,
In each other's hearts, we learn to fly.

Melodies played in perfect sync,
Time slows down, we rarely blink.
In shared rhythms, our spirits thrive,
Tuning into joy, we come alive.

Echoes of friendship in every beat,
Comfort found in moments sweet.
Across the distance, we stand as one,
In the music's warmth, our fears are shunned.

Through ups and downs, we cling and sway,
In the dance of life, we'll find our way.
With every song, our souls converge,
Tuning into love, we always emerge.

So let us gather, let the music play,
In togetherness, come what may.
With open hearts, we'll always know,
Tuning into joy, together we'll grow.

Reflections in the Digital Mirror

Screens display fragments of who we are,
Reflections captured, near and far.
Pixels shimmer with tales untold,
In this digital realm, we dream bold.

Caught in moments, we laugh and cry,
Snapshots of life as time rushes by.
Each filtered glance, a story shared,
Mirrored souls, unmasked and bared.

Behind the glare, we seek the truth,
Searching for wisdom in fleeting youth.
In our screens, our lives unfold,
Reflections of hearts, both brave and bold.

Through virtual lenses, we connect and part,
Woven in threads, we play our part.
Underneath the surface, emotions stir,
In digital mirrors, we gently blur.

So let us ponder what lies beneath,
In reflections found, we form our wreath.
Through screens we wander, yet long to hold,
Reflections in the mirror, stories unfold.

Messages in Bottles

Drifting on waves, hopes intertwined,
Messages in bottles, love defined.
Secrets whispered to the restless sea,
Carried far from you to me.

Each bottle holds a dream or wish,
Floating gently, like a lover's kiss.
With every tide, new stories arise,
In the ocean's arms, our hearts will rise.

Letters penned with ink of hope,
Navigating currents, love's long scope.
In ocean depths, our hearts will roam,
Messages in bottles, leading us home.

So cast your dreams upon the waves,
In sunlit glimmers, our spirit braves.
Let hope be cast, let kindness flow,
Messages in bottles, let love grow.

Together we'll sail, through storm and calm,
With every message, we find our balm.
In watery whispers, our union swells,
Messages in bottles, where love dwells.

Echoes of Laughter

In the park where children play,
Giggles dance in light of day.
Joyful sounds, a sweet refrain,
Echoes linger, love's domain.

Whispers soft like summer breeze,
Laughter flows with playful ease.
Memories bright, a warm embrace,
Time stands still, in this place.

Underneath the starry sky,
Laughter sparkles, soaring high.
Moments cherished, hearts unite,
Every sound a pure delight.

In the echoes of the night,
Laughter glows, a guiding light.
Together, we will always stand,
The rhythm of our hearts so grand.

Through all storms, through thick and thin,
In laughter's arms, we all begin.
To dance beneath the silver moon,
In harmony, forever tune.

Pixels of the Heart

In a world of bits and bytes,
Emotions painted in cool lights.
Every pixel tells a tale,
Of love that will never pale.

Swipe through memories so bright,
Captured moments, pure delight.
Each image holds a story true,
Connecting me, and me to you.

Through screens, our feelings flow,
In vibrant colors, love will grow.
Every gesture, every smile,
Bridging gaps across each mile.

As we share each little part,
We stitch together, heart to heart.
Through pixels, we paint our fate,
Crafting wonders, never late.

In this gallery we hold tight,
Foundations built in digital light.
For every click, a cherished start,
A vivid dream of pixel art.

Threads of Affection

Woven soft with gentle care,
Threads of love are always there.
Stitched together, moments shared,
In this fabric, hearts are bared.

In each knot, a memory sewn,
In every loop, affection grown.
Colorful strands, tight and bright,
Together we create our light.

Through the storms and sunny days,
These threads bind us in tender ways.
Even when the world feels cold,
Our love's warmth will never fold.

With every touch, the fibers strain,
Strengthening what we can't contain.
Weaving stories, life expressed,
In this tapestry, we are blessed.

So hold on tight, let the world know,
These threads of affection continue to grow.
Bound by love, forever entwined,
In this creation, peace we find.

The Art of Touching Hearts

A gentle touch, a fleeting glance,
Awakens in us all a dance.
With subtle grace, we share our souls,
In quiet moments, love unfolds.

Words unsaid, yet understood,
In simple gestures, we find good.
Each heartbeat echoes through the air,
An artful way of showing care.

Soft caress, or warm embrace,
Transforms a life, leaves a trace.
Every smile, a brush of light,
Painting shadows, making bright.

Together we create a song,
In harmony, we both belong.
Through every touch, we find our part,
The beauty in a touching heart.

So let us treasure every sign,
In the art of hearts entwine.
With every moment that we share,
A masterpiece crafted with care.

Transparency in Shadows

Beneath the veil of night, we tread,
Secrets linger where fears are fed.
Flickers of truth in flickering light,
Guiding the heart through the depths of fright.

Whispers echo in the empty room,
As clarity fights off the looming gloom.
Every shadow has a story to tell,
In the silence, we begin to dwell.

Fragments of honesty peek from the dark,
Illuminating pathways, a gentle spark.
In the dance of contrasts, we find our way,
Bringing forth hope as we greet the day.

With each step taken, the past unravels,
Momentum built from tiny travels.
We seek the light that shines so bright,
In transparency, we find our might.

Affection in the Algorithm

Numbers dance in calculated grace,
Connecting souls in a digital space.
In binary code, emotions bloom,
Crafting a language where hearts consume.

Through screens we share the laughter and tears,
Bridging the distance across the years.
Patterns twist in romantic code,
As affection grows, corruption erodes.

Data flows like a river wide,
In the algorithms, we confide.
Love encrypted, yet plain to see,
A paradox that sets us free.

Navigating paths through electric streams,
We forge connections, pursue our dreams.
In circuits and wires, there's warmth to feel,
Creating bonds that time can't steal.

Each interaction, a spark divine,
In pixels' embrace, our souls entwine.
Amidst the codes, the heart finds a way,
Affection grows more with each passing day.

Notes from the Niche

In the quiet corners, whispers bloom,
Crafted tales dispelling the gloom.
Hidden truths in a scattered script,
A symphony where the unheard crypt.

Each niche alive with vibrant hues,
As forgotten voices seek to muse.
In shadows cast, the light finds ink,
Recording moments before they sink.

Threads of stories weave through the air,
Coloring lives with tender care.
In every note, a world unfolds,
In the unseen, our heartache molds.

From the margins, we break the norm,
Gathering warmth in each silent storm.
In niches, we find our brave refrain,
Understanding that joy often comes with pain.

Through solitude, connections arise,
Finding solace where wonder lies.
Each note a step into the divine,
In the niche of life, our dreams align.

Lighthouses in the Data Sea

In the vast expanse where numbers drift,
Lighthouses gleam, guiding us swift.
Through stormy bytes and endless streams,
We search for meaning in digital dreams.

The waves of data crash and roll,
Yet steadfast beams help navigate the soul.
Each flicker of light, a promise so bright,
Leading us home through the shadowed night.

Signals pulse, like heartbeats alive,
In the chaos of code, we find a drive.
Finding direction in seas unknown,
Together we forge our path, our own.

As bytes become stories, rich and vast,
We grasp for a future while honoring the past.
In every query, in every search,
We're lighthouses shining, ready to urge.

Among the data, we stand as one,
In the sea of bytes, our journey begun.
Navigating through the noise and the fear,
Lighthouses gleam, forever near.

Patterns of Togetherness

We weave our dreams in gentle light,
Colors blending, side by side.
Through laughter shared and tears we fight,
In every heartbeat, love's our guide.

In shadows deep, we find our way,
With whispers soft, we touch the skies.
Through every night and brightening day,
Together strong, our spirits rise.

In quiet moments, hands entwined,
The world outside cannot divide.
In every glance, our hearts aligned,
Through thick and thin, we stand with pride.

With every story, we grow near,
In every silence, words unspoken.
Through every joy and shaded fear,
Our bond unbreakable, never broken.

So let us dance beneath the stars,
While time flows gently, tides of fate.
In patterns formed, like constellations,
Together always, never late.

The Soundtrack of Our Lives

In every note, a memory sings,
A melody of hopes and dreams.
With rhythms soft, our heartbeat clings,
In every silence, the echo beams.

Through different paths, our tunes align,
The highs and lows, a symphony.
In laughter bright, the stars we find,
A harmony, you and me.

As seasons change, the music flows,
A dance of joy, a waltz of pain.
Within our hearts, the chorus grows,
In every storm, the sweet refrain.

So let the world create its sound,
With every step, we find our way.
In every beat, true love is found,
Together still, come what may.

The soundtrack plays through night and day,
In every heart, a song unique.
With every note, we'll gently sway,
Our life's great tale is all we seek.

Adventures in Pixels

Within the screen, new worlds collide,
Adventures born from bits of light.
With every click, our hopes abide,
In pixel dreams, we take to flight.

Through digital realms, we boldly roam,
From puzzle quests to battles won.
In coded lands, we find our home,
Together chasing endless fun.

With every frame, a story told,
Each curve a journey deep and vast.
In colors bright, our hearts unfold,
In every game, a bond is cast.

Through dungeons dark and skies so clear,
We conquer fears, we face the night.
In laughter shared, we chase the cheer,
In every moment, pure delight.

So here we'll sit, in pixel glow,
Our adventures weave like threads of fate.
In every quest, our spirits grow,
Together, coding memories great.

Coded Compassion

In every line of code we write,
Compassion grows, a guiding hand.
With empathy, we share the light,
In every heart, a promise stands.

Through screens aglow, we learn to care,
With every click, we break the wall.
In virtual realms, our voices share,
Together strong, united all.

In every program, kindness streams,
A digital touch to heal the soul.
With open hearts, we dare to dream,
In every space, we feel the whole.

So let us code with love and grace,
In every byte, a chance to grow.
Through every challenge, we embrace,
A world where kindness overflows.

In harmony, we weave the trust,
Through every project, hand in hand.
With coded hearts, we rise, we must,
In every line, together stand.

Melodies of Shared Dreams

In twilight's glow, we find our song,
Notes intertwine, where we belong.
Hearts resonate, in soft embrace,
A harmony that time can't erase.

Echoes of laughter, memories bright,
Guiding us through the silent night.
With each whisper, a promise made,
In every heartbeat, fears will fade.

Winds of change, they softly call,
Unfolding stories, one and all.
In every challenge, strength we share,
Together, we face what life may dare.

Amidst the stars, our dreams take flight,
Emerging colors from the night.
With open hearts and hands held tight,
Our symphony shines, pure and bright.

Journeying Together in Bits

Step by step, we walk this road,
In tiny pieces, our stories flowed.
Through ups and downs, we learn with grace,
Finding connection in every place.

Bits of laughter, stitches of tears,
Crafting a path that silences fears.
In shared moments, we find our way,
Creating memories day by day.

Navigating maps of hopes and dreams,
Together, we shine, like sunlight beams.
Each fragment a chapter, carefully penned,
Writing a tale that will never end.

As pixels merge, our essence blends,
Through every twist, our journey extends.
Side by side, through thick and thin,
In shared bits, our souls begin.

Flashes of Understanding

In quiet moments, clarity strikes,
Just like lightning, it ignites.
Words unspoken bridge the gap,
In fleeting glances, truth unwraps.

Within the chaos, we find a spark,
Illuminating paths once dark.
In shared silence, wisdom speaks,
Through simple gestures, connection peaks.

Ephemeral truths, like stars aglow,
Guide our hearts, teaching us to grow.
In every pause, a lesson starts,
Building bridges between our hearts.

With every flash, we come to know,
The depths of love, how deeply it flows.
In understanding, we find our way,
Through life's challenges, come what may.

Dancing Within Pixels

In digital realms, we sway and twirl,
Crafting moments, a vibrant swirl.
With every click, our spirits rise,
In this dance, we find our skies.

Colors flicker, bright and bold,
Stories shared, both new and old.
In pixelated joy, we intertwine,
Creating memories, yours and mine.

Through screens we laugh, through screens we cry,
In virtual spaces, we learn to fly.
With glowing hearts, we break the norm,
In colorful dances, our dreams transform.

Every frame tells a tale unique,
In rhythmic beats, our spirits speak.
Together we move, in cyberspace,
Dancing forever, in this shared place.

Laughter Across Distance

Across the miles, a chuckle rings,
Echoes of joy on whispering winds.
Bright memories weave between us still,
A bond unbroken by time or will.

Through screens we share our silly grins,
In every jest, a spark begins.
Though far apart, our spirits dance,
With laughter found in every chance.

Moments stolen in fleeting chats,
Every smile makes up for the flat.
As distance fades, together we glow,
In laughter's warmth, we always grow.

Distance may stretch, but hearts connect,
In every jest, there's love reflected.
With laughter's thread, we stitch our fate,
Bridging the gaps, we celebrate.

So let the miles remind us sweet,
Of joy that makes our lives complete.
In every giggle, our song will play,
Together forever, come what may.

The Language of Connection

Words unspoken weave through the air,
In silent glances, feelings share.
A smile, a nod, they speak so loud,
Binding us close within the crowd.

In every heartbeat, a rhythm flows,
The language of love, it gently grows.
With every touch, our spirits align,
Two souls in dance, by fate's design.

Across the noise, we find our beat,
A melody that makes us complete.
Through the chaos, we hear the song,
In connection deep, where we belong.

With every laugh and every sigh,
In the spaces we share, we learn to fly.
The language of hearts, a precious find,
In the silence, true love is blind.

So let us cherish every sign,
In whispered words, our dreams entwine.
Together we'll weave a tale so rare,
In the language of connection, we dare.

Shared Sunsets and Ifs

As twilight spills its golden hues,
We watch the sun set, lost in views.
With every glow, a promise made,
In shared sunsets, memories cascade.

Underneath the vastening sky,
We ponder dreams and wonder why.
In whispered hopes, and soft, sweet ifs,
Together we drift, the world lifts.

Each color blooms, an artist's stroke,
In moments shared, our hearts invoke.
With every dusk, we paint our dreams,
In twilight's glow, nothing's as it seems.

Bound by the hues of day's last light,
In conversations deep into the night.
With shared sunsets, every doubt clears,
In laughter and love, we cast our fears.

So let the sky hold our secrets tight,
In every dusk, our spirits ignite.
Through shared sunsets and ifs we find,
A journey together, eternally aligned.

Colliding Worlds

When our paths crossed, stars did align,
Two worlds collided, a dance divine.
In the chaos, we found our way,
A melody born from night and day.

With every whisper, sparks took flight,
Igniting dreams in soft moonlight.
Together we forged a brand new tale,
In colliding worlds, our love prevails.

The galaxies spun with every smile,
As time stood still, just for a while.
Through cosmic journeys, hearts entwined,
In this vast universe, you are mine.

Amidst the noise, a tranquil place,
In your embrace, I find my grace.
With dreams we chase and hopes unfurled,
In the magic made, we change the world.

So here we stand, no fear to fight,
In colliding worlds, all feels right.
Together forever, we'll chart the skies,
In love's embrace, our spirits rise.

When Screens Fade

In the silence, whispers stay,
Faded echoes of yesterday.
Thoughts drift like leaves in the breeze,
As time weaves moments with ease.

Pixels dim and hearts align,
Memories etched, love's design.
When the glow begins to wane,
True connections remain the same.

Fragments of light, a passing phase,
Life beyond the glowing gaze.
Each flicker, a story told,
In the warmth of memories bold.

The world outside, a vibrant scene,
While screens dim and lose their sheen.
We find solace in the real,
As forgotten lights softly heal.

Gathered here in twilight's grace,
Finding comfort in each embrace.
As screens fade, our hearts ignite,
In the stillness of the night.

Lifelines through Lenses

Through lenses clear, we see the light,
A world alive, bold and bright.
Connections bloom with every frame,
Lifelines forged, we share the same.

Every click, a moment caught,
In laughter lived, in battles fought.
Glances exchanged, so rich, so rare,
Through these lenses, souls laid bare.

Time stands still in fleeting sights,
Each snapshot holds our heart's delights.
In the depths, our stories flow,
Through reflections, our spirits grow.

Captured smiles, a fleeting glance,
In digital realms, we find our chance.
Life unfolds beneath our eyes,
As dreams ascend to painted skies.

A tapestry of friends and foes,
In every lens, a journey flows.
Through lifelines forged in pixel's art,
We find our way, never apart.

Unwritten Letters of Strength

In pages blank, our souls await,
Unwritten words, a silent fate.
Strength lies beneath the silent pen,
In every drop, we rise again.

Letters lost in time's embrace,
Stories woven without a trace.
Yet in their absence, courage grows,
In whispered hopes, the heart bestows.

Pages flutter under unseen hands,
As we write, life's grandest plans.
Each line a memory, raw and rare,
Unspoken truths, laid bare with care.

Through ink and dreams, we pave the way,
Where light breaks through the longest day.
Strength in silence, a powerful tone,
In unwritten letters, we find home.

In every pause, our voices ring,
Life unfolds, revealing spring.
With every word, we mend our seams,
Unwritten strength, the heart's true dreams.

The Warmth of Shared Screens

In the glow of friendship's light,
Screens aglow, hearts take flight.
Together here, we laugh and cry,
In this space, our spirits fly.

Shared moments flicker, stories weave,
In pixels bright, we dare believe.
Each message sent, a lifeline cast,
In shared screens, time moves fast.

Through the lens, we bridge the miles,
In every chat, a thousand smiles.
Connections forged in twilight's gleam,
In shared screens, we find our dream.

As light dances on faces near,
In this space, we conquer fear.
Every shared laugh, a heart's refrain,
In this warmth, we rise again.

When distance calls and nights grow long,
In shared screens, we still belong.
Together, we thrive, our hearts so keen,
In this glow, our love is seen.

Connections in the Digital Age

In a world of screens, we meet,
Fingers tap in rapid beat.
Voices echo through the wire,
Hearts connect, ignite the fire.

Distance fades, we share our days,
In shared laughter, in silly ways.
A click, a post, a heartfelt thread,
Bridging gaps where silence bred.

Though faceless, we still embrace,
In this vast, electric space.
Moments shared, though miles apart,
Digital warmth ignites the heart.

Through the noise, we seek the clear,
In shared stories, joys appear.
With every ping, a pulse anew,
Connections spark, creating crew.

So let us cherish, bits and bytes,
Found in pixels, pure delights.
In the canvas of the night,
We weave our dreams, a shared insight.

Threads of Light

In a tapestry of stars, we weave,
Glowing threads where hopes believe.
Each flicker tells a tale of old,
Of dreams chased and hearts bold.

Through the night, our spirits roam,
Finding solace and a home.
Woven binds, both near and far,
Illuminate where wishes are.

With every stitch, a memory made,
Silken ties that never fade.
Colors blend, in harmony sing,
Uniting voices, hope they bring.

From shadows cast, we rise anew,
Threads of light in every hue.
A dance of souls, in pure delight,
Guided by the threads of light.

So take my hand, let's journey far,
Through the cosmos, where dreams are.
In the fabric, we will find,
The unity that binds mankind.

Echoes of Laughter

In rooms so bright, the laughter rings,
Echoes dance on playful wings.
Moments cherished, joy so sweet,
A symphony of hearts that beat.

Through open doors, the fun spills wide,
Every chuckle, a cherished ride.
In gentle jests, we find our place,
Warmth felt in each smiling face.

Whispers loud in silent nights,
Candle's glow, our hearts ignite.
Shared stories make the shadows fade,
In laughter's light, our fears betrayed.

Together we create the sound,
In every moment, joy is found.
With every giggle, every cheer,
The echoes carry, drawing near.

So let us laugh 'til daylight breaks,
In every heart, the joy awakes.
Together, in this sweet refrain,
Echoes of laughter, our love's gain.

Pixels of Togetherness

Every pixel forms the scene,
Moments shared, where we've been.
Frames and filters, colors bright,
A collage of life, pure delight.

In this space, we come alive,
A symphony of souls that thrive.
Click and capture, memories freeze,
A world connected, hearts at ease.

Through the grid, our stories blend,
In every frame, a message send.
Captured smiles and tears we share,
A community that's always there.

As pixels dance, our spirits soar,
In digital realms, we explore.
Together in this vivid art,
United, though apart, we start.

So let's embrace this vibrant race,
In every pixel, find our place.
Hand in hand, though worlds apart,
Pixels of togetherness, we chart.

The Bridge of Shared Stories.

In twilight's gentle glow we stand,
With tales that bind our hearts and hands.
A bridge of whispers, hopes collide,
In every story, we confide.

Through laughter's echo, sorrows fade,
A woven path where dreams are laid.
Each word a step, each pause a breath,
Together we conquer life and death.

Like rivers flowing side by side,
In the tapestry of life, we bide.
From every joy and every tear,
We've built a bond that knows no fear.

The stitches of memory hold us tight,
In darkness, we find shared light.
With every chapter, our spirits soar,
On this bridge, we're forevermore.

So tell your stories, let them flow,
In this embrace, we come to know.
Across the miles, the years, the strife,
Our bridge shall carry the gift of life.

Silent Connections

In quiet moments, we reside,
Where words are lost, but hearts confide.
A glance, a sigh, a fleeting smile,
Silent connections bridge the miles.

Through tangled thoughts and whispered dreams,
In fragile bonds, our spirits gleam.
No need for sounds, our souls align,
In silent depths, our hearts entwine.

We share our fears, our deepest aches,
In stillness, a bond that never breaks.
With every pause, we find our song,
A melody that feels so strong.

As shadows dance beneath the stars,
These silent ties erase our scars.
With every heartbeat, every breath,
In quietude, we conquer death.

So in the silence, hold me near,
Within our hearts, there's warmth and cheer.
Each unspoken word a sacred thread,
In silent connections, love is fed.

Digital Bonds

In pixelated spaces, souls collide,
Through screens that glow, our hearts abide.
A tap, a swipe, a world unknown,
In digital threads, we've all been sewn.

From distant lands, we gather 'round,
In this vast web, our voices found.
Words unspoken travel so fast,
In every moment, hold the past.

Our laughter shared in gifs and memes,
A tapestry woven from our dreams.
With just a click, we're never alone,
In digital realms, we've carved our throne.

Through shadows cast by city lights,
We forge our paths on sleepless nights.
With every message, a spark ignites,
In digital bonds, we've set new sights.

So let us dance in this online sphere,
Together we rise, bound without fear.
In bytes and bits, our hearts expand,
In this universe, hand in hand.

Whispers Across the Screen

In soft glow of screens, our whispers glide,
Across the expanse, where feelings bide.
With every keystroke, hearts unfold,
In typed embrace, our stories told.

Through blinking cursors, secrets shared,
In quiet corners, we're unprepared.
With every sentence, trust we weave,
In virtual realms, we dare believe.

Like shadows fleeting, our thoughts take flight,
In whispered tones, we find the light.
With every pause, a tension grows,
In shared silence, our longing shows.

As distance fades and time stands still,
These whispers echo, strong and shrill.
Holding close what words can't express,
In our connection, we find the rest.

So let them flow, these whispers sweet,
In every heartbeat, we retreat.
Across the screen, we build our dreams,
In whispered breaths, love redeems.